CHILDREN'S ROOM

J 972 ARD   JUN 1 3 2001   FELDHE

Ardagh, Philip.
Aztecs
2000.

P9-EGL-184
SAN BERNARDINO PUBLIC LIBRARY

4 9876 00033 7937

39 2008(9-08)

HISTORY DETECTIVES

AZTECS

DISCARD

Ripped/loose
page 101519 DS
damage
noted

CONTENTS

THE AZTECS

The Aztecs lived in the country we now call Mexico, in Central America. It is a hot place of deserts, volcanoes and mountains. Many people imagine that the Aztecs were around thousands of years ago, at the time of the Ancient Egyptians, but this isn't true. The Aztecs didn't settle in the Valley of Mexico until the 1320s and their empire was destroyed by the Spanish in the 1520s. That's less than 500 years ago.

Statues found in the ruins of the Great Temple in Tenochtitlan (now Mexico City).

THE FIRST PEOPLE

Different groups of people have lived in Mexico over time. Some had gone long before the Aztecs arrived. Others shared some of their history with the Aztecs.

The Olmecs (about 1200BC–400BC) were the first major group to live in Mexico. They made amazing carvings — a tradition carried on by others in Mexico for thousands of years afterwards.

Another mighty people were called the Toltecs (about AD900–1150). At one time, most of central Mexico was under their rule. Their name means "artists" but they were great fighters too.

The Mayas (about 300BC–AD1540), who were still living in the area at the time of the Aztecs, are famous for their fantastic cities and their complicated system of picture writing.

The position and size of the Aztec Empire in 1519

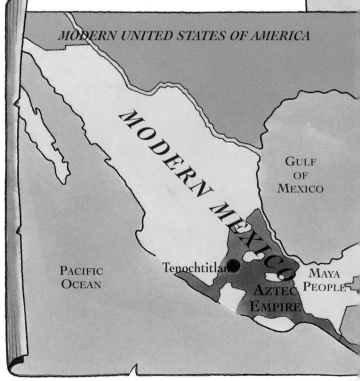

MODERN UNITED STATES OF AMERICA

MODERN MEXICO

GULF OF MEXICO

PACIFIC OCEAN

Tenochtitlan

AZTEC EMPIRE

MAYA PEOPLE

The Valley of Mexico

Tula

LAKE
TEXCOCO

Teotihuacan

Tenochtitlan

causeways

The ruins of
the temple
at Teotihuacan.

POPOCATEPETL
VOLCANO

CARIBBEAN
SEA

The eagle symbol for the
Aztec capital, Tenochtitlan.

THE AZTECS ARRIVE

The Aztecs arrived in the Valley of Mexico in about 1250. According to Aztec legends, they were originally a small tribe from Aztlan in western Mexico. Aztlan means "place of herons." The legend says that the Aztecs were guided by the gods, who told them to settle when they saw a good omen — an eagle standing on a cactus with a snake in its talons.

The eagle was seen on a swampy island in the middle of Lake Texcoco, so it was here that the Aztecs made their home.

In truth, it's far more likely that there wasn't much room in the Valley of Mexico, so the first Aztecs had to settle on land which no one else wanted, in the middle of a lake.

Whatever the reason, the Aztec settlement in Texcoco grew into the city of Tenochtitlan. And, as it grew, so did the power of the Aztecs. Soon they had an empire of millions.

DISCOVERY

In 1446, swarms of locusts ate the crops, leaving the Aztec people starving. These Aztec pictures come from the Aztec book, the Codex Florentino.

This serpent, with a head at either end, is a brooch made up of a mosaic of tiny pieces of turquoise. Rich from their conquests of neighboring peoples, important Aztecs wore fine jewelry. This was probably worn by a priest.

FAMOUS NAMES

Probably the most famous name in Aztec history is Moctezuma (also spelt Montezuma) — a name shared by two different Aztec rulers. Moctezuma I, who ruled from 1440 until about 1468, did much to help the beginnings of the Aztec empire, whereas Moctezuma II was one of the last of the Aztec Emperors.

THE ANGRY GODS

Moctezuma I's reign began with one disaster after another. There was a plague of locusts, serious floods and a series of bad frosts and failed crops — which led to terrible famine. Aztecs were dying of hunger in huge numbers, and it was thought the disasters were caused by angry gods. Moctezuma I decided to offer the gods more human sacrifices than ever before. He revived the War of the Flowers to capture more prisoners for sacrifice, and to enlarge the empire.

THE SPREAD OF POWER

As Moctezuma I's warriors invaded more and more lands, they forced the defeated peoples to pay regular tribute — which could be anything from animal skins to jewelry — to their new Aztec masters. Moctezuma I died in about 1468, a hero to his people, who had been made far richer by these conquests.

A NEW LEADER, A NEW TEMPLE

In 1486, another famous name emerged: that of Ahuitzotl who became emperor then until 1502. He came to power just before the Great Temple in the capital city of Tenochtitlan was finished in 1487. To celebrate this event, there was a four-day festival of human sacrifices. Some say that over 20,000 humans were killed as offerings to the gods. Ahuitzotl killed the first victim. He also led his people in many wars to capture more sacrificial prisoners and riches and to expand the empire.

FOOD, FLOODS AND TENOCHTITLAN

As the Aztec population grew under Ahuitzotl, more food needed to be grown to feed the people, and more fresh water needed to be channeled to the crops. Tenochtitlan (see pages 12 and 13) was badly flooded by water from these channels in 1500 and many houses and floating crop gardens were destroyed. It was under Ahuitzotl that a new city was built out of the old — far greater and more impressive than ever before.

MOCTEZUMA II

Probably the most famous Aztec is Moctezuma II, emperor from 1502 to 1520. His reign ended in disaster and the downfall of the Aztec empire. He was defeated by the Spanish forces of Hernán Cortés, who conquered the Aztecs in 1521. (See pages 38 and 39.)

HOW WE KNOW

Historians and archeologists (people who dig up and study things from the past) have learned a great deal about Aztec life from the writings and drawings, and from the items they left behind. Throughout this book, there are "discovery boxes" showing just some of the artifacts that still survive today and help us to learn more about the Aztecs.

DISCOVERY

The Great Temple at Tenochtitlan, finished by Ahuitzotl, was the most important temple in the Aztec empire. This fine example of a pyramid-shaped temple can still be seen in Teotihuacan but is much smaller than the Great Temple.

Moctezuma II gave the Spanish many gifts when they arrived, including gold, jewels and featherwork. This head-dress is a fine example of Aztec featherwork. It is made of gold and decorated with tall green feathers and shorter blue, pink and brown feathers.

CITY IN THE SWAMP

Tenochtitlan, the Aztecs' greatest city, grew from just a handful of huts on a rock in a swampy lake called Texcoco. It was joined to the mainland by three raised paths — or causeways — made out of earth, volcanic rock and stone.

Everything had to be carried across them on foot. The Aztecs didn't have horses, asses or mules and didn't use handcarts because they hadn't discovered such uses for the wheel.

As well as thousands of homes, the city was filled with schools, markets and temples. But, instead of having streets, people and goods traveled along a network of canals.

Tenochtitlan was not only an amazing feat of building and design, it was also the heart of the Aztec Empire of about 11 million people.

As the years passed, the city of Tenochtitlan grew bigger, spreading further across Lake Texcoco.

The palace and the Great Temple were in the center.

In an emergency small wooden sections of the causeways could be knocked aside to keep out invaders.

The busy causeways were the only way to and from the city without using a canoe.

12

This volcano was called Popocatepetl. It means "smoking mountain."

Most houses were one story high to protect them against regular earthquakes.

Chinampas, sometimes called "floating gardens," were small fields built by the farmers from mud and reeds.

People often traveled to and from the city in flat-bottomed canoes.

DISCOVERY

This sixteenth-century engraving is of the plan of Tenochtitlan drawn for the Spaniard Cortés, who first set foot in the city in November 1519. He was greatly impressed by the size of Tenochtitlan but he was horrified by the human sacrifices.

This colorful picture was painted by an Aztec artist in the sixteenth century. In the center is the symbol of the city — an eagle perched on a cactus with a serpent in its claw. This was the legendary sign from the gods telling the Aztecs that this was the place to build their city.

WRITING AND THE CALENDAR

The Aztecs created their own picture writing — the kind of writing that experts call hieroglyphs. The pictures stood for sounds from their spoken language, Nahuatl, and for whole objects. By the sixteenth century though, some symbols stood for whole ideas too. For example, a footprint didn't mean a footprint, it meant travel.

Aztec hieroglyphs were also carved into stone to make calendars. Calendars were a very important part of Aztec life because religious ceremonies were connected to time and the seasons.

The Aztecs believed that the world they lived in was the fifth world and that the four before it had been destroyed. The destroyers were jaguars, wind, fire and water. The Aztecs believed that their own world would also be destroyed one day — by earthquakes.

The Aztecs had two types of calendar — religious and everyday. Their everyday calendars divided the year into 365 days. Religious calendars, like this one, divided the year into 260 days.

wind

fire

Calendar stones were brightly painted. Each of the twenty days had a different hieroglyph. The twenty days made one "month."

Some Aztec hieroglyphs:

knife

death

movement

monkey

rabbit

14

Some calendar stones were over 9 feet across and weighed more than 24 tons!

jaguar

The sun god was at the center

water

Years went in special 52-year cycles. These cycles were counted by adding a special stick to a bundle of sticks at the end of each year—until 52 had been collected.

The bundle was then burned and a new cycle began.

DISCOVERY

The Aztecs wrote in codices. These are books which unfold into one long strip instead of being made up of lots of different pages. A single book is called a codex. This codex—the Codex Fejervary Mayer—is made of deerskin. It tells the stories of Aztec gods and people.

This is a carving of 52 "year sticks" in a bundle. The Aztec hieroglyph in the middle is the name of the final year of the cycle. At the end of this year the bundle was burned in a religious ceremony.

GODS AND GODDESSES

Tlaloc, god of rain and food, was half human and half alligator. His name means "Lord of all water sources."

The Aztecs worshipped hundreds of gods. When they conquered a new tribe, they took over that tribe's gods and worshipped them too. They believed that everything in life was "fated." This meant that whatever happened to a person was decided by the gods.

One of the most important gods was Huitzilopochtli, the god of war and the sun. The Aztecs believed that the sun wouldn't rise in the sky every morning, unless this god was offered human blood every day.

One of the two shrines at the top of the Great Temple at Tenochtitlan was dedicated to Huitzilopochtli. The other was dedicated to Tlaloc, the god of food and rain. Thousands of people were sacrificed in their names.

Huitzilopochtli, the god of war and the sun. The name actually means "The hummingbird on the left." In the afterlife, warriors killed in battle became hummingbirds.

Quetzalcoatl, "The feathered serpent," was god of the winds and of priests.

16

Mictlantecuhtli, "Lord of the realm of the dead," was, as his name suggests, god of the dead. His head was like a human skull.

Chicomecoatl, the goddess of maize, protected the seeds and crops. Her name means "Seven serpents."

Chalchiuhtlicue, the goddess of water, looked after lakes and rivers. Her name means "Our lady of the turquoise skirt"—a skirt which looked like flowing water.

DISCOVERY

This carving of Coatlicue, the earth goddess, was discovered in Mexico City in 1790. She represents the hardships of life. Her skirt is made of writhing serpents, her necklace of hands and hearts, and she wears a human skull on her belt.

This stone mask is of Xipe Totec, the god of spring. He is wearing gold "ear plugs"—the Aztec form of stud earrings!

17

PYRAMID TEMPLES

The Aztecs built pyramids but, unlike the more famous Ancient Egyptian ones built thousands of years earlier, these were temples and not tombs. An Aztec temple had step-shaped sides and a huge staircase up the front.

The most famous temple was the Great Temple in the middle of Tenochtitlan. It was rebuilt on the same site six times, getting bigger and better each time.

The main use for the temple was as a place to hold ceremonies in honor of the gods. During some festivals, hundreds of people were sacrificed. Some had their hearts cut out, some were shot with arrows and some had their heads cut off.

The Aztecs believed that the gods needed these blood sacrifices to live and without them the world would come to an end. It was a great honor to be sacrificed to the gods.

This was the shrine to Tlaloc, the god of food and rain.

The chacmool was a statue of a "messenger" holding a bowl. The victims' hearts were probably placed in here.

This inner chamber was filled with offerings to Tlaloc, the water god. These included sea shells, fish carvings and water pots.

There were also offerings of human skulls.

When the Great Temple of Tenochtitlan was at its biggest and grandest, it reached a height of 98 feet.

18

This was the shrine to Huitzilopochtli, the god of war and the sun.

sacrificial altar

Temple priests were not allowed to cut or wash their hair.

Noblemen attended important ceremonies at the temple.

Victims were led up the temple steps.

In one four-day ceremony, many thousands of victims were sacrificed.

DISCOVERY

Knives such as this one were used to sacrifice victims. The razor-sharp blade is made from flint and the handle, in the form of a crouching man, is a mosaic of different stones, including turquoise.

This picture from a codex shows a priest cutting out a victim's heart. Later, the victim's skull would have been put on show on a special rack for skulls.

THE AFTERLIFE

The Aztecs believed in reincarnation—that they would be reborn, but not as the same person. In fact, probably not as a person at all. What they came back as depended on how they died, not what they had done when they were alive.

It was believed that most people ended up in Mictlan, the realm of the dead, ruled over by the god Mictlantecuhtli. This was the place for those who died of natural causes. On the journey to Mictlan, the dead people's skin was ripped off by a wind of knives so they would reach Mictlan as skeletons. Once there, they had to dance with other living skeletons until it was time to be born again.

Warriors who died in battle, however, were sent to the Eastern Paradise, ruled over by the sun god in the sky. After four years of fighting pretend battles in a garden of flowers the dead warriors came back to life as butterflies or hummingbirds. The god of war's name (Huitzilopochtli) means "hummingbird on the left."

This temple was pyramid-shaped.

The pointed roof was made from reeds.

The entrance to this sanctuary was carved with a mask shaped like the open jaws of a serpent.

The altar was shaped like an eagle. Behind this a small circular hole was cut into the floor. This was for offerings of blood to the gods.

The temples at Malinalco were dedicated to two types of noble Aztec warriors: the eagle warriors and the jaguar warriors.

The lower half of the temple was carved into the solid rock of the hillside.

Offerings were thrown into firepits and burnt as gifts to the gods and goddesses.

This temple contained the firepits.

Eagle warriors and jaguar warriors hoped to die in glorious battle and go to the Eastern Paradise.

DISCOVERY

This turquoise ceremonial mask is of Quetzalcoatl, the god of winds, priests and of learning. It is a brilliant example of the Aztec art of mosaic making.

This frightening-looking pottery figure, with a grinning skull-like head, represents Mictlantecuhtli, the god of death.

WARRIORS AND WAR

Most men spent a number of years in the army, and could be called up again to fight at any time. The Aztecs were nearly always at war and, although they weren't paid, it was a great honor to be a soldier. A man couldn't officially be a warrior until he had taken three enemies prisoner. After that, he could even have a special warrior haircut! If he took four or more prisoners he could become a nobleman.

Aztec warriors captured all these prisoners because they needed them as human sacrifices. They believed that without sacrifices the sun wouldn't rise every morning.

The more prisoners a warrior took, the more elaborate clothing he could wear. Jaguar warriors wore jaguar skins and were sent off to spy on the enemy. Eagle warriors dressed like eagles with beaked helmets and feathers. They looked terrifying and made loud frightening noises when attacking. Many noblemen were full-time soldiers.

A good Aztec warrior didn't kill, but captured the enemy.

arrow warriors

A maquahuitl was part club and part sword. Its edges were made of razor-sharp obsidian.

A wooden spear-thrower, called an atlatl, made it possible to launch spears much higher and further.

jaguar warrior

eagle warrior

22

In an emergency, 100,000 Aztec warriors could be called up to fight.

Quilted suits made good armor. They were soaked in salt water to make them hard.

Shields also helped protect the Aztec warriors.

Aztec officers wore feather "standards," strapped to their backs. This showed that they were in charge.

the warrior haircut

Like the arrow tips, spearheads were edged with a razor-sharp rock called obsidian, a kind of natural glass.

DISCOVERY

This ceremonial shield is decorated with a mosaic of different colored feathers, showing a blue creature with a long tail on a red background.

An Aztec warrior's most important job was to capture prisoners for sacrifice. The more prisoners he took, the higher his rank became. This codex shows the most junior warrior top left and the most senior warrior bottom right, wearing the most elaborate uniform to show how important he is.

TRADE AND THE MARKET

Aztec merchants had privilege and power. They could get very rich but this was against laws, so they had to try to keep their wealth a secret. They dressed in ordinary clothes in public and sneaked their goods into Tenochtitlan under the cover of darkness.

Merchants traveled far and wide. Some trade missions could last years. Merchants often had to disguise themselves when in foreign countries so that people didn't know they were Aztecs. Some actually spied for the army.

Most everyday buying and selling for ordinary people took place in market places across the Aztec empire. In Tenochtitlan you could buy everything from fruit, fish and vegetables to pottery, baskets, gold, glue and even slaves — but meat was very rare. People usually paid for things with cocoa beans, not money.

Many slaves wore wooden collars.

Slaves were sold on a raised platform.

materials

baskets

All goods were carried by people. Aztecs didn't use donkeys, mules or horses. They didn't use the wheel, either.

fruit and vegetables

food stall

24

Many goods in Tenochtitlan were given in "tribute" (a kind of tax) by other cities.

Only rich nobles could wear the finest brightest clothes.

Merchants brought back luxury goods.

Merchants' children could only marry the children of other merchants.

Merchants setting off on trade missions often took soldiers with them for protection.

DISCOVERY

16,000 rubber balls, shields, and bundles of feathers are just some of the many items recorded on this official list of the "tribute" sent to the Aztecs in Tenochtitlan as a kind of tax from conquered lands.

Pots, such as this one, were bought or bartered for at the market. They were used for cooking, eating and for storage. The Aztecs didn't have potter's wheels so they shaped the pots by hand.

FUN AND GAMES

Fun and games didn't necessarily go together. Tlachtli, the sacred ball game, was taken very seriously indeed and very few goals were ever scored. Then there was the flying dance which was an early form of bungee jumping, but with an important religious meaning. Four men, dressed as birds, jumped from a pole with rope tied to their ankles. As the rope unwound around the pole the men spun outwards.

Music and dancing were also important parts of Aztec life and were taught at school. Pipes, rattles and drums were played at most religious ceremonies. Large conch shells were used as trumpets to summon troops. Some festivals included hundreds of dancers.

tlachtli court

Tlachtli players could not touch the ball with their hands.

Players wore padding on their knees and arms.

Patolli was a popular game, played with a dice and counters made from beans and pebbles.

Players often gambled and they offered prayers to the god Macuilxochitl for good luck.

pipe player

dancers

26

Spectators watched tlachtli from the top of the high walls.

Tlachtli balls were made of hard rubber.

drummer

Flying dancers were dressed as birds.

DISCOVERY

If a ball passed through a stone ring, such as this one, on a tlachtli court, a goal was scored. The rings were attached high on the court wall in an upright position, not sideways like a basketball hoop.

Shaped like a turtle, this is actually a simple wind instrument called an ocarina. It was held in both hands and blown into to make simple low notes.

27

THE ROYAL PALACE

The emperor's royal palace was built on two levels on the edge of the Temple Precinct in Tenochtitlan. It was enormous. It was more than just a home for the Great Speaker—or Huei Tlatoani—as the emperor was sometimes called. The upstairs apartments were for him and his family, but downstairs was home for thousands of servants, as well as a jail, weapons room, treasure store and law courts. There was even a zoo in the palace!

There were many gardens filled with sweet-smelling flowers, and the roof was inlaid with scented cedar wood. Some historians have suggested that this was to try to cover up the horrible smells which drifted from the nearby temples!

It was against the law to walk barefoot in the palace. The punishment was death.

Huge royal palaces were built for the emperors.

roof garden

Over 20,000 Aztec pancakes, or "tortillas," were eaten in the palace every day. Many provisions were brought in by canoe.

The windows had no glass, but brightly colored curtains kept out the heat.

28

The emperor's private apartments were on the upper floor.

guards

The council chamber was on the ground floor.

canal

DISCOVERY

The Aztecs loved flowers and the emperor's gardens were filled with them. There was even a god of flowers — Xochipilli — shown on this carving. His name means "Flower Prince" and he was also the god of poetry and dance.

This picture of the palace shows the emperor Moctezuma II in his throne room. The men below are his counselors, seated in the council chamber. His war counselors met in the room (shown empty) on the bottom left.

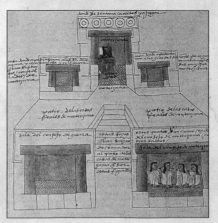

29

LAW AND ORDER

flaming torches

The Aztec people were grouped into clans called calpulli, and the calpulli courts settled minor disputes. There was a higher court to settle more serious matters. There were very strict rules and laws about almost everything in Aztec life—down to what a person could or couldn't wear.

Thieves usually had to pay back twice what they stole, or become slaves. Drunks had their heads shaved the first time they were caught, but were executed if they were caught again. Cutting down a living tree was also punishable by death, and murderers were sacrificed to the gods.

The greatest sin of all, however, was treason—betraying the emperor and the empire. A traitor lost all he owned, his land was destroyed, his children were sold into slavery and he was killed.

Minor cases were held in local courts.

They were judged by senior warriors.

30

The most important cases were heard in the emperor's palace in the Aztec capital.

It was rare for the emperor himself to pass judgement.

The judges' assistants sat behind them.

Judges wore special head-dresses in court.

Cases were heard by four top judges.

The accused knelt before the judges.

Witnesses had to swear in the name of the god Huitzilopochtli that they would tell the truth.

DISCOVERY

This picture, taken from a codex, shows an executed criminal. He was put to death by stoning. The Aztecs executed their criminals in many different ways.

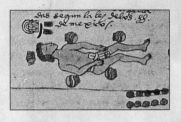

Here we see four judges deciding the fate of six criminals — three men and three women. The men behind the judges are their assistants.

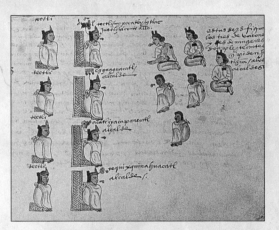

FARMING AND FOOD

Poor people in Tenochtitlan had to farm small plots of land built on the lake. These "floating gardens" were chinampas. They were built up with reeds and mud, and were held in place by stakes cut out of willow. On these the farmers grew maize (corn on the cob) and vegetables, kept turkeys and fished.

Most people ate maize "porridge," beans and tortillas. Meat was mainly for the rich. Fruit and vegetables included avocados, tomatoes and chillies. Aztecs liked their food to be spicy.

Rich people drank chocolate, made from cocoa beans and honey, and an alcoholic drink called pulque, made from the maguey cactus.

Life for farmers on Tenochtitlan was much harder than for those on the mainland with their bigger, drier fields.

Ordinary people's houses could only be one story high. They usually had two rooms.

Walls were built from mud and plaster.

Willow stakes were hammered deep into the bottom of the lake.

Farmers didn't own their land. It belonged to their clan, or calpulli.

Tree roots help to keep the chinampas in place.

32

maize store

Parrots were used to raise the alarm (as we use guard dogs today).

Flat clay discs were used as cookers for tortillas (maize flour pancakes).

reed mats

The fertile soil was dug with carved digging sticks.

DISCOVERY

This statue is of a farmer carrying maize in a basket on his back. He is gripping a strap which runs around his head and helps to hold the basket in place, in traditional Aztec style.

This jug, made from a white mineral called calcite, has been carved into the shape of a hare. Only rich Aztecs would have owned such fine objects. They probably used them to serve drinks such as pulque, made from cactus juice.

33

CLOTHES AND JEWELRY

Clothes played a very big part in Aztec life. What you wore showed just how important you were and there were very strict rules. Most men wore plain loincloths and cloaks. Most women wore plain tunics and skirts. Noblemen and women could wear brightly colored clothes—but any ordinary people caught wearing such clothes were put to death. That was the law.

Colored feathers were worn by important officials, warriors and priests during ceremonies. Jewelry was popular amongst the rich. They wore jewelry made from gold, turquoise and jade.

Ordinary people's clothes were made from the fibers of the maguey cactus. They were very rough.

Rich noblemen wore brightly colored cloaks. Their loincloths were colorful too.

A warrior commander could wear his cloak below the knee, and a feather head-dress.

maguey cactus

Noblemen and noblewomen had clothes made from cotton.

Sandals were often made from the skin of jaguars.

34

Important men, as well as women, wore jewelry including gold pendants, ear "plugs" and sometimes even nose and lip jewelry.

Cloaks were fastened with a knot. Aztecs didn't use pins.

Women wore tunics.

Aztecs didn't grow cotton so it was bought from foreign lands.

DISCOVERY

These beautifully carved pieces of pottery were used by an Aztec woman to print patterns on her face. They were covered in different colored dyes and then pressed on to her skin.

Most Aztec gold jewelry was melted down by the Spanish after the invasion by Cortés. This impressive piece of Mixtec jewelry is from the same period and survived the Spanish plunder.

LIFE AS A CHILD

Life for an Aztec child was very strict. Parents were very happy to have children, but wanted to prepare them for the tough life ahead. Naughty children were often pricked with cactus spikes. Naughty girls were sometimes given extra housework instead.

Schools were free. Most children went to schools called telpochcalli. Here children learned history, religion and even music and dancing. Children of the nobles went to a different kind of school, called a calmecac. They were taught math, astrology, law, medicine and writing as well as other skills for their future life of nobility. The boys were trained to be brave warriors.

Some boys were chosen to go to real battles, carrying provisions for the adult warriors.

At a telpochcalli, the boys were taught to be brave warriors.

Both girls and boys learned dancing and music.

Girls learned to spin and weave cactus fibers.

Younger children were taught at home.

Most girls married and looked after the home.

36

A common punishment for failing a test at a calmecac was having your head shaved.

Children of nobles, at the calmecac

Although the clubs were only wooden, children were sometimes injured.

Wrestling was also important to build up strength and confidence.

Punishment included being held over the stinging smoke of burning chillies.

DISCOVERY

A punishment popular with parents and unpopular with children was to hold a child over the smoke from burning chilli peppers, as shown in this codex.

Girls could marry when they were fifteen. This picture of a wedding, also from a codex, shows the bride twice — being carried into the

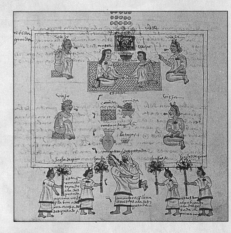

groom's house and then with her clothes knotted to the groom's. "Tying the knot" was an important part of the Aztec marriage ceremony.

MOCTEZUMA AND CORTES

Moctezuma II, Emperor of the Aztecs 1502–1520

Hernán Cortés, leader of the Spanish conquistadors

In 1502, Moctezuma II became ruler of the mighty Aztec empire. As emperor, he strengthened his power and conquered more lands, and the Aztec people became even richer.

In 1504, meanwhile, a Spanish merchant ship sailed to the Americas. On board was an 18-year-old Spaniard named Hernán Cortés, eager to find adventure ... and gold. In 1511 he set sail again, to Cuba where the Cubans were defeated. Cortés became Secretary to the new Spanish Governor.

THE CONQUISTADORS

But Cortés wanted new adventures. In 1519 he set sail for Yucatan in Mexico where there were reports of great riches. He traveled with 550 soldiers, called conquistadors. Here, Cortés heard about the powerful Aztec civilization to the west, and sailed further along the coast. He made friends with local people, exchanged gifts, and sent messages to Moctezuma II at Tenochtitlan that he would like to meet him.

TO THE CITY IN THE SWAMP

Joined by thousands of the Aztecs' enemies — tired of having to pay tribute to the Aztecs — Cortés's forces headed inland to Tenochtitlan.

When they finally reached the capital of the Aztec Empire, in November 1519, Cortés was stunned. He had hoped to be able to conquer the Aztecs easily ... but here was a city far greater and grander than anything in Spain.

THE MEETING AND BETRAYAL

The Aztecs had never met anyone like the Spanish before. They'd never seen pale-skinned people, armor or horses. Many thought that these newcomers must be gods. Cortés and his men were made welcome, gifts were exchanged, and the Spanish were invited to stay in the palace. But

Moctezuma II was taken prisoner and forced to swear loyalty to Spain.

When Cortés went to the coastal city of Vera Cruz in May 1520, he took the Aztec emperor with him. While he was away, Cortés left the conquistador Alvarado in charge. Alvarado — horrified by the Aztecs' human sacrifices and frightened of being attacked himself — had his men slaughter many Aztecs at a religious ceremony. This made the Aztecs rise up against the Spanish, swearing to kill every last conquistador on Aztec soil.

The Aztecs set eyes on the Spanish for the first time.

THE MEETINGS BETWEEN CORTÉS AND MOCTEZUMA II, AS RECORDED BY THE SPANIARD BERNAL DÍAZ DEL CASTILLO

> *Each bowed deeply to the other ... Cortés brought out a necklace of elaborately worked and colored beads which he hung around the great Moctezuma's neck ... Moctezuma had some fine gold jewels in a variety of shapes ... which he gave to Cortés ...*
>
> *(On another occasion) Cortés gave his usual greetings, then said to Moctezuma: "If you cry out or cause any disturbance, you will be killed immediately by my captains ..."*

THE DEATH OF MOCTEZUMA

On his return to Tenochtitlan, Cortés tried to get matters back under control by having Moctezuma II speak to his people. Unfortunately, many Aztecs felt that the emperor had betrayed them to the Spanish. They stoned Moctezuma to death.

Cortés and his conquistadors were forced to flee the city across the causeways. In the bloody battle that followed in the darkness, huge numbers of lives were lost on both sides.

It wasn't until August 13, 1521, after Cortés's forces besieged the city for three months, that the Spanish gained control of Tenochtitlan and the Aztec empire was at an end.

Spanish and Aztec forces battle it out on one of Tenochtitlan's causeways.

DISCOVERY

Cortés and his men were presented with many gifts when they first arrived in the Aztec Empire. Here Cortés is being given a necklace.

Very few pieces of gold Aztec jewelry remain, most having been melted down by the Spanish.

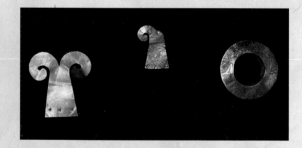

These thin golden ornaments have, however, survived. They would have been worn through the nose and ears.

DISCOVERING THE PAST

Archeologists are people who study the past, often by digging up and looking at things which have been left behind. They are true History Detectives, piecing together the clues left by earlier peoples, to try to build up a picture of how they used to live. In the study of the Aztecs, these clues range from the smallest pieces of pottery to jewels, codices, statues and carvings.

TOOLS OF THE TRADE

Like modern police services, archeologists now have many pieces of scientific equipment to help them in their detective work. By using special equipment to measure how much carbon there is in an object, for example, they can work out how old the object is. This test is called carbon dating.

ARCHEOLOGY OF THE AZTECS

Much of what the Aztecs created was destroyed or plundered in their lifetime. After the Spanish invasion by Cortés, gold jewelry was melted down, and temples and buildings were pulled down. Most of the stones were reused to create new buildings, which means that important clues about the Aztec way of life have been lost.

MEXICO CITY

Because Mexico City was built on the site of the Aztec city of Tenochtitlan, archeologists haven't been able to carry out many excavations. Some important discoveries have been made by accident, though. In 1978, for example, workmen working near the Metropolitan Cathedral in Mexico City dug up a huge stone disc on the site of the Great Temple at Tenochtitlan. This chance find renewed interest in the temple and, as a result, archeological teams excavated the area.

PICTURE PUZZLES

Two of the most useful sources of information about the Aztecs are their own richly illustrated codices, and reports written by the Spanish invaders. The codices show scenes from all different aspects of Aztec life from childbirth to life after death, with everything else in between. Some of the most dramatic adventures leading to the fall of the Aztec empire, however, were written down by Cortés's companion Bernal Díaz del Castillo, including their first meeting with Moctezuma II.

THE SPOKEN WORD

Many people living in Mexico today still speak a version of the Aztec language, Nahuatl. In fact, a number of Aztec words have become words in other languages too. For example, the Aztecs used to eat two kinds of food that were only found in what we now call Mexico. One was "chocolatl" and the other was "tomatl." Not only are these now eaten and enjoyed all over the world, you can also see where the words "chocolate" and "tomato" come from.

DISCOVERY

These statues were unearthed by archeologists in the remains of the Great Temple in what was once Tenochtitlan and is now Mexico City. They are statues of Aztec people and not gods.

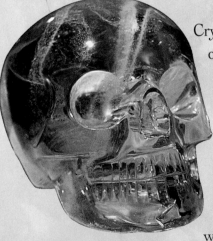

Crystal skulls, like this one, were thought to have been made by Aztecs to represent Mictlantecuhtli, the god of death. Some people later claimed that these sacred artifacts were cursed. It has now been discovered that at least some of the crystal skulls are modern fakes.

41

TIMELINE

The city of Tenochtitlan founded in about 1345.

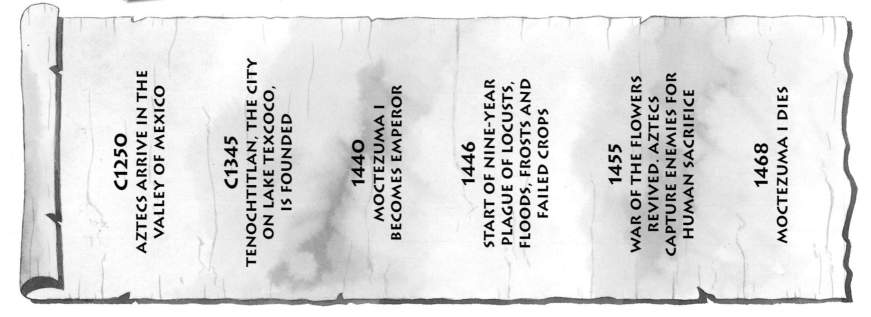

C1250
AZTECS ARRIVE IN THE VALLEY OF MEXICO

C1345
TENOCHTITLAN, THE CITY ON LAKE TEXCOCO, IS FOUNDED

1440
MOCTEZUMA I BECOMES EMPEROR

1446
START OF NINE-YEAR PLAGUE OF LOCUSTS, FLOODS, FROSTS AND FAILED CROPS

1455
WAR OF THE FLOWERS REVIVED. AZTECS CAPTURE ENEMIES FOR HUMAN SACRIFICE

1468
MOCTEZUMA I DIES

c. is short for "circa," which means "about."

The Aztecs were made rich by their conquests.

Gold jewelry from the conquered Mixtecs.

A mosaic mask. The Aztecs were great craftsmen as well as warriors.

42

The Aztecs and the Spaniards fight on the causeways of Tenochtitlan.

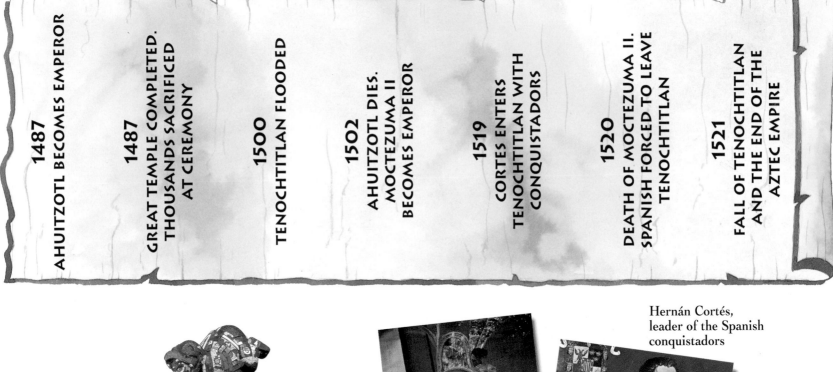

1487
AHUITZOTL BECOMES EMPEROR

1487
GREAT TEMPLE COMPLETED. THOUSANDS SACRIFICED AT CEREMONY

1500
TENOCHTITLAN FLOODED

1502
AHUITZOTL DIES. MOCTEZUMA II BECOMES EMPEROR

1519
CORTES ENTERS TENOCHTITLAN WITH CONQUISTADORS

1520
DEATH OF MOCTEZUMA II. SPANISH FORCED TO LEAVE TENOCHTITLAN

1521
FALL OF TENOCHTITLAN AND THE END OF THE AZTEC EMPIRE

An Aztec sacrificial knife

Emperor Moctezuma II

Hernán Cortés, leader of the Spanish conquistadors

YOUR MISSION

WELCOME TO TENOCHTITLAN: THE FABULOUS CITY ON THE LAKE AT THE HEART OF THE AZTEC EMPIRE. IT WAS FROM HERE THAT TROOPS OF THE MIGHTY GENERAL FIRE WIND LEFT TO ATTACK A VILLAGE. THEIR TASK WAS TO CAPTURE VILLAGERS TO BE SACRIFICED TO THE SUN GOD AND TO BRING BACK RICHES.

THE VILLAGERS KNEW THAT THE TROOPS WERE COMING. THIS WAS NO SECRET, WITH THE HUGE ARMY APPROACHING BY THE HOUR, AND THE LOUD BEATING OF THE DRUMS . . . BUT A SPY FROM AMONGST THE AZTEC FORCES TOLD THE VILLAGERS OF THE GENERAL'S ACTUAL PLANS. RATHER THAN FIGHTING WITH HONOR, THE VILLAGERS WERE ABLE TO SLIP AWAY INTO THE NIGHT, BEFORE THE ATTACK AT DAYBREAK, TO AVOID CAPTURE.

YOUR MISSION IS TO FIND THE ENEMY SPY.

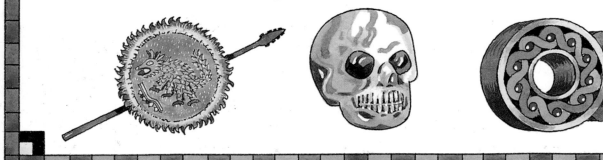

HOW TO BE A HISTORY DETECTIVE

To help you solve the mystery, you will need to answer questions along the way. These can be answered by using information from the first half of this book. Simply turn to the page number shown in the magnifying glass.

For example, **12** would mean that an answer lay somewhere on page 12.

These answers also earn you points, so that you can keep score. You'll find how many points an answer scores when you check yours against the answers on pages 58 and 59.

But you must do more than simply answer the questions to find out who is the enemy spy. You must look out for clues in the words and pictures, too.

By the end of the story, you should be able to say who the spy is. You can find out if you're right by checking page 60. The right solution will score you an extra 20 points.

Add up all your points and find out how good a history detective you are (also on page 60).

Good luck!

YOUR MISSION BEGINS

Hurrying past warriors in splendid head-dresses, their obsidian-edged spears glinting in the midday sun, you come face to face with General Fire Wind. He is standing in the heart of the enemy village, but with no forces to fight against. The place is deserted.

"Gone!" he cries with rage. "All gone, apart from a few stragglers." He jerks his head in the direction of a handful of villagers being led away. "Betrayed! I've been betrayed. One of my own people must have warned them of my plan . . . and *you* are to find the culprit."

47

STONE KNIFE   FEATHER WING   RAIN FLOWER

Fire Wind brings his wooden club crashing down in front of you, and you shudder. "Only three other people knew the exact plan of attack on this enemy village," he roars. "Stone Knife, the priest who advised me, Feather Wing, an eagle warrior, and Rain Flower, the cook who served us as we made plans yesterday evening in the priest's quarters."

At that moment, the three suspects are brought to the general. The priest glares at Fire Wind with blazing anger in his eyes. The eagle warrior stares straight ahead, impassive, like a true soldier. The cook looks down at her feet. She looks nervous in front of such important people.

"One of you will pay for this crime," snarls the general. "The crime is treason . . . and you all know what the punishment is." What is it? **30**

Back in Tenochtitlan, you make your way to the home of General Fire Wind where you are to stay as his guest during your investigation. This is a great honor. You wander out on to the rooftop and look out over the city.

A girl appears at your side, with a big grin on her face. "Hello," she says. "I'm Sky, the general's daughter. Do you need any help trying to track down the enemy spy?"

You look surprised.

"Oh, don't worry. My father tells me everything," Sky explains. "I'm not a child. Next month I'll be old enough to marry."

So how old is Sky? **37**

She tells you how much she wishes girls were allowed to join the army, too. "I think I'd make an excellent warrior!" she says, leading you back inside.

A servant hurries into the room. "I have just been given an important message," he tells you. "You are to go to the market by the Temple Precinct. You must meet with the Masked Serpent beneath the symbol of the city. There you will learn important information for your investigation."

Sky dashes out into the street to see if there's any sign of the messenger . . . but there's no one about.

"How very strange," sighs Sky. "Are you going to go to meet the Masked Serpent?" she asks. "It could be a trap!"

"It could be important," you reason. Now all you need to do is figure out the meaning of *the symbol of the city*. What is it? **13**

The market is packed full of people. It is rich with the smell of spices and full of noise and color.

"Look out for the symbol of the eagle and the cactus," you remind her, but—after what seems an age—you're the one who finally spots the Masked Serpent. The turquoise mask is made of fine mosaic. Who does the mask represent? **21**

"I am witness to important events," says the Masked Serpent. "The night before General Fire Wind and his army attacked the enemy village, I saw Feather Wing, the eagle warrior, slip out of camp and head towards the village."

"You think that makes him the enemy spy?" protests Sky. "Perhaps he was spying *for* my father and not sneaking off to give away plans."

You know that can't have been the case. Why? **22**

"And why didn't you report this to the general at the time?" you demand.

"It didn't *mean* anything at the time," whispers the voice. "It was only after the attack failed, and I heard rumors of an enemy spy, that I realized it might be important."

"Then what have you got to hide?" asks Sky. "Why not show yourself?" As quick as a flash, she tries to snatch the disguise, but the Masked Serpent is even quicker. Sky finds her wrist in the tight grip of the Masked Serpent's left hand.

"I've said enough," whispers the mysterious stranger, who then turns and, without warning, dashes off. Sky follows.

You chase after them but the masked stranger has already been swallowed up by the crowds of shoppers. After a hopeless search, you see a familiar face. Rain Flower is with a group of men carrying baskets of food from the market.

You ask her if she's seen anyone in a mosaic mask, and she nods eagerly. "I saw someone with a turquoise mask, running towards the Great Temple," she says, "but they weren't dressed like a priest, so I thought it was a bit odd." She looks down at her own clothes. "Like me, you can tell they are not of noble birth," she says. What does she mean? **34**

With a wave to the cook, you and Sky now dash to the Great Temple. On the steps you meet yet another of your suspects: Stone Knife. He looks pale and is sweating. You wonder whether he's unwell or hiding a guilty secret. You're about to ask him if he's seen anyone in a mask when he speaks.

"You've come to question me, at last," he says climbing the steps. "I am, of course, innocent. We need captured villagers to sacrifice to the gods. Why would I risk making the gods angry by warning the enemy and giving them the chance to escape? Some fools only fear the Great Speaker, but it is the gods we should all fear the most!"

The Great Speaker? Who does he mean? **28**

A cry goes up from below. There is a commotion at the foot of the temple and shouts from the shoppers. You scramble back down the temple steps to investigate.

THE CHASE IS ON

The furious priest, Stone Knife, strides down the steps after you just as a boy — a very familiar boy — darts between legs, around bodies and through crowds of bemused shoppers, hotly pursued by two soldiers.

It takes you a moment to remember where you've seen him before. Of course! He was one of the few stragglers left behind in the enemy village and captured by General Fire Wind's men. Now he's wearing a wooden collar. What does this mean? 24

He could have some important information about who the spy is. You join in the chase and, for the second time this morning, find yourself running through the market.

You lose sight of him a couple of times, but have more success than when you hunted for the Masked Serpent.

You see the boy making a dash for a walled area, where groups of people are watching some event.

What is this place? 26

You scan the people to see if there is any sign of the boy and catch snatches of conversation from those around you.

"There's talk of a secret group helping slaves escape from the city," says an old man.

"And people who are waiting to be sacrificed," says a woman. "No good will come of it! It'll make the gods angry, and we'll all be in trouble, mark my words."

Distracted by what you've overheard, and pushed from all sides by the growing crowds of onlookers now that the tlachtli is reaching an exciting climax, you give up hope of ever finding the escaped slave boy.

"Look!" says Sky, pointing at one of the tlachtli players. "That's Feather Wing, the eagle warrior. I'd recognize him anywhere with that huge scar across his cheek."

"He's a good player," you say, watching him.

"He's supposed to be the best," agrees Sky. "My father says that he has the strongest right arm in the game!"

With the game over, Feather Wing's team leave the tlachtli court to the cheers of the crowd. He catches sight of you.

"Surely you haven't come to interrogate me here?" he protests, sweat pouring from his brow. You tell him that you've met someone claiming to be a witness who saw him creeping out of the camp on the night before the attack.

"They're either lying or mistaken," groans Feather Wing. "We eagle warriors look much alike when in our uniforms."

"Your scar makes you easy to recognize," Sky points out.

The warrior looks down at Sky sadly. "I've known you all your life, Sky," he says, "and you know how much I respect your father." She nods.

"He is a great general and a great soldier. No one handles an atlatl better than he used to," the warrior adds, "but I also thought he was my friend . . . and friends don't accuse each other of spying."

What's an atlatl?

You are suddenly (22) distracted . . . you've caught sight of the escaped slave boy. The chase is on again!

Sky launches herself at the boy but he slips through her fingers and dashes into one of two buildings . . . it's impossible to tell which.

You enter the first building and find yourself in Rain Flower's kitchen. She is preparing tortillas — maize flour pancakes — for the warriors.

She recognizes you. "Did you catch the Masked Serpent?" she asks. You shake your head. "You think it was me who warned the enemy about the attack, don't you?" she sighs.

When you explain that you're simply on the trail of a runaway slave boy, Rain Flower assures you that you're the first person to come in or out of here since

she got back from the market. You look around just the same, in case the boy somehow managed to slip in here unnoticed. "Is there anything you can tell me about the night before the attack?" you ask as you search.

"Nothing out of the ordinary," she says, "except I saw Feather Wing, the eagle warrior, leaving camp. I expect he was on some important mission."

"You're the second witness to say you saw that," says Sky, appearing in the doorway. She's searched the other building — a food store — and there's no sign of the escaped slave in there. "But I did find this hidden there," she says. What is it? **19**

The next morning, the beat of the war drum summons all the soldiers in the city to the Temple Precinct. The sun shines down on the thousands of men, ready to go off to war. General Fire Wind is addressing his troops.

"Ours is a glorious task," he bellows. "For those of us who come back to Tenochtitlan, it will be with sacrifices for the altars of Huitzilopochtli . . . for those of us who do not return, it will mean fights amongst the flowers!"

There is a loud roar as the men cheer their leader. What does the general mean by "fights amongst the flowers?" **20**

You look around you, knowing that all three suspects are among the warriors, priests, cooks, musicians and boys from the telpochcallis helping to carry the weapons. The general is a man who believes in having the suspects near him so that an eye can be kept on them.

The march lasts for many hours, and when camp is finally set up at the end of a long hard day, it's time to put your latest plan into action.

Disguised as a kitchen helper, Sky carries baskets full of provisions backwards and forwards and keeps watch on the cook.

You're disguised as a soldier in a uniform of padded armor lent to you by the general in the hope that you can get closer to the eagle warrior and the priests without scaring them off. You catch sight of Stone Knife who is lurking in the shadows with someone you don't recognize.

TROUBLE IN THE CAMP

Creeping as close as you dare to Stone Knife and the stranger, you strain to hear what they're talking about.

"How are you feeling?" asks the stranger, cheerfully.

"Better, but do keep your voice down, doctor," urges Stone Knife. "Others might think it a bad omen if they knew I — their chief priest — was unwell at this time."

"Don't worry," says the doctor. "They're all afraid of you, old friend."

"They wouldn't be if they knew

that I was almost asleep on my feet when the general told us his plans just before that failed attack on the village!" hisses the priest. "Your sleeping herbs were too strong. I was asleep the moment they left my quarters. I'm surprised they didn't hear my snores!"

"Don't worry. I won't tell Fire Wind that you slept right through until daybreak," says the doctor.

"It's the gods I'm worried about," says Stone Knife. "Perhaps they were angry with me and . . ."

Just then Feather Wing, the eagle warrior, appears in a rage. "Rumor has it that you, Stone Knife, are accusing me of being that wretched traitor they call the Rabbit," he fumes. "The one who warned those villagers of the attack, and who leads the secret group that helps slaves escape from Tenochtitlan!"

"The Rabbit?" whispers Sky, who has been listening, too.

"Haven't we seen a rabbit symbol somewhere already?"

Right now, all you can think about is sleep after such a long day's march, but your head is reeling with all the new information you've overheard. You find a spot near Stone Knife and settle down.

Then you notice a symbol has been drawn in the dirt next to his sleeping form. What does it mean? **14**

Before you have time to think, a figure comes leaping through the air — weapon in hand — and raises a spear above the startled priest. The glinting, razor-sharp tip is thrust forward, narrowly missing his body.

The attacker runs away, with you, the priest, Sky and other angry soldiers in hot pursuit.

The attacker reaches the edge of the camp and leaps over a rocky ridge, out of view. There is a cry of pain.

Scurrying over the ridge, you find Feather Wing, lying unconscious on the ground, still clutching his spear in his right hand.

"The fool!" says Stone Knife. "He fails to assassinate me, runs away, falls and then knocks himself out! This man has no honor. This is the Rabbit, your enemy spy."

Just then, Rain Flower the cook appears. "Is he the spy?" she asks, looking down at the unconscious eagle warrior. "Have our names been cleared at last?"

Sky turns to the cook. "What are you doing up and about at this time of night?" she asks.

The cook holds up a cactus. "Gathering cacti to make pulque," she says.

What is pulque? 32

Apart from a sore head, Feather Wing, the eagle warrior, now seems to be fine . . . not that he expects to live for much longer.

He and the two other original suspects are with you and Sky, standing before General Fire Wind.

"I didn't try to attack Stone Knife, sire," the eagle warrior protests. "If I had, I wouldn't have missed."

"Perhaps your knock on the head has conveniently allowed you to forget what you did!" says the priest.

The two men glare at each other.

"The evidence is very much against you," says Sky's father. "I have reports that Rain Flower, the cook, saw you leave camp on the night you heard my plans!"

"That's not true," says Feather Wing. "She is either mistaken or lying to protect herself."

"But an informer called the Masked Serpent told us the same story—that you crept out of camp under the cover of darkness," the general points out.

"But why would I betray our people?" reasons Feather Wing. "I've been a loyal subject of the Emperor all my life."

Fire Wind turns to you. "I take it that you are satisfied that Feather Wing is none other than the traitor they call the Rabbit and the enemy spy who warned the villagers of our plans?" he asks.

That's a good question, but not necessarily an easy one to answer. Just because things look bad for Feather Wing doesn't mean it has to be him. It doesn't mean it can't be him either.

Who is the enemy spy? Feather Wing, Stone Knife or Rain Flower?

You can check your answer with the SOLUTION on page 60

ANSWERS AND SCORES

Next to each answer is a number. This is the number of points you should award yourself if you got the answer right without looking it up here in the back first. And there are extra points if you worked out who is the enemy spy.

PAGES 48 & 49

- Traitors lose everything they own. Their land is destroyed, their children are sold into slavery and then they are put to death.   6 points

- Sky must be fourteen, coming up to fifteen years old. That's when Aztec girls can marry.   6 points

- The symbol of the city of Tenochtitlan is of an eagle clutching a snake while perched on a cactus. There's a woman standing in front of such a painted symbol.   5 points

- The mask is of the god Quetzalcoatl, the feathered serpent.   6 points

- It is a *jaguar* warrior's job to spy. The eagle warrior's job is to attack the enemy with as much noise as possible.   6 points

PAGES 50 & 51

- There are strict rules as to what people can wear. Nobles wear colorful cloaks. The Masked Serpent and Flower Rain, the army cook, are both dressed as commoners.   6 points

- The Great Speaker—which in Aztec is the "Huei Tlatoani"— is another name for the emperor or king, the most famous of whom was probably Moctezuma II.   5 points

- Wooden collars, such as the one around the boy's neck, are worn by some slaves. The fact that this particular boy is running suggests that he's escaped.   6 points

- It is a tlachtli court, where the ball game tlachtli is played.   5 points

PAGES 52 & 53

- An atlatl is a wooden device used by warriors for throwing their spears further.   5 points

- This is a ceremonial knife used by priests to sacrifice human victims to the gods.   6 points

PAGES 54 & 55

• If a warrior dies in battle, he fights mock battles in a garden
of flowers in the Eastern Paradise, until he comes back to life
as a butterfly or a hummingbird.   6 points

• This is the Aztec hieroglyph for "DEATH."   6 points

PAGES 56 & 57

• Pulque is an alcoholic drink made from the maguey cactus.   6 points

A MESSAGE TO ALL WOULD-BE
HISTORY DETECTIVES

Add up your score so far, before you turn the page
to find out who the enemy spy is . . .

When you've checked the solution, score an extra
10 points if you guessed the right person.

Score **20 points** if you worked out who the spy
was by spotting all the clues.

SOLUTION

Stone Knife, the priest, could not be the spy. He had taken sleeping herbs and fallen asleep moments after the plans were discussed, and didn't wake up until daybreak (page 55). We know that the attack itself was made at daybreak (page 46), the day after the plans were made (page 48), so he couldn't have warned the enemy. There was no time.

Things look bad for Feather Wing, the eagle warrior, but he didn't attack the sleeping priest (page 56).

The person in the eagle warrior uniform was holding the spear in their left hand . . .	. . . The unconscious figure of the real Feather Wing was clasping his spear in his right (page 56).	Feather Wing had been knocked out and left behind the ridge earlier . . . the imposter then attacked Stone Knife.	. . . leapt over the ridge, let out a cry and then hid, waiting for the real eagle warrior to be found.

Rain Flower, the cook, is left-handed (page 55), and so is the Masked Serpent (page 50). Both claimed to have seen Feather Wing sneaking out of camp on the night the general revealed his plans. In fact, they are one and the same person.

By pretending to be two different people, Rain Flower was backing up her own account and making it doubly believable. She made the mistake of asking if you'd caught the Masked Serpent (page 55) but you hadn't mentioned the person in the mask by name when you spoke to her earlier at the market (page 50), so how could she have known it? There's also a piece of the Masked Serpent's clothing sticking out of one of Rain Flower's helper's baskets (page 50).

We know that "the Rabbit" not only warned the villager's of the plan of attack, but also leads a secret group helping slaves escape (page 55). There is the Aztec symbol for "rabbit" on the kitchen wall behind Rain Flower (page 55) and a collar similar to the one worn by the escaped slave boy (page 52) is in the kitchen (page 55).

Rain Flower claimed no one else had been in her kitchen, but there were wet footprints by a knocked over water jar (page 55) — left by someone in bare feet, but she was wearing sandals. She had hidden the priest's knife in the food store so she could plant it as evidence against Stone Knife if needs be.

When Sky asked her what she was doing after the attack on the priest (page 56), Rain Flower claimed to be gathering cacti to make pulque. Pulque is made from the maguey cactus (page 32), which has long thin leaves, unlike the kind she's holding. In fact, she'd just slipped out of her eagle warrior uniform and rubbed the fake scar off her face. Rain Flower is "the Rabbit," the enemy spy.

HOW DID YOU DO?

BETWEEN 90 AND 100 POINTS Wow! When it comes to being a History Detective, you're the very best. You're not only good at following the clues, but you worked them all out brilliantly. Well done. **BETWEEN 75 AND 89 POINTS** Excellent! You're true detective material. You worked well with the facts to solve the clues. **BETWEEN 60 AND 74 POINTS** Not bad. Not bad at all. You've got some way to go before you're a truly great detective, but you certainly know how to handle an investigation. **BETWEEN 50 AND 59 POINTS** OK, so you're not going to win any big-shot detective awards, but you're on your way to becoming a pretty good detective. Keep practicing! **LESS THAN 50 POINTS** Oh dear. A short spell at detective school wouldn't do any harm. Better luck next time.

GLOSSARY

Atlatl — a wooden spear thrower, designed to make it possible for a warrior to launch a spear much higher and further than if he simply threw it with his arm.

Calmecac — a school for the children of noblemen and noblewomen.

Calpulli — Aztec clans. Members of a clan were all related to each other. Calpulli courts settled minor disputes within their own clans.

Causeway — a strip of land built over water. Causeways were built across Lake Texcoco connecting Tenochtitlan to the mainland.

Chacmool — the carved figure lying at the entrance to the shrine to Tlaloc on top of the Great Temple at Tenochtitlan. The reclining statue "holds" a stone pot into which blood offerings were poured.

Chinampas — small fields, often called "floating gardens," built up of reeds and mud on lakes.

Codex (plural: Codices) — an Aztec book that unfolded into one long strip, instead of being made up of many different pages. When stored, it was folded like a concertina.

Conquistadors (sometimes spelled Conquistadores) — conquering Spanish soldiers of the 16th century.

Maguey Cactus — a spiny long-leaved cactus used by the Aztecs for making **pulque**, and to weave into material to make clothes.

Maquahuitl — half sword, half club, this looked like a short wooden paddle with blades made from obsidian embedded in the edges.

Mosaic — a decoration created by joining together small pieces of stone or shell. Turquoise mosaic jewelry was highly prized by the Aztecs.

Nahuatl — the language spoken by the Aztecs. It is still spoken in parts of Central America.

Obsidian — a volcanic rock which is a kind of natural glass. It was easy to sharpen and was used by the Aztecs to make blades.

Patolli — a popular game played with pebbles. People usually gambled on who would win.

Pulque — an alcoholic drink made from the maguey cactus.

Telpochcalli — a **calpulli** school for ordinary children, rather than those of nobles who attended a **calmecac**.

Tlachtli — a ball game played between two teams. To score a goal, a hard rubber ball had to pass between a stone ring without the player using his hands.

Tortillas — pancakes made from maize flour and filled with different fillings.

Tribute — goods, that could be anything from feathers to gold or food, which had to be given to the Aztec Empire by conquered cities.

Turquoise — a bluish-green semi-precious stone.

War of the Flowers — a ceremonial combat. The aim was to take as many captives as possible for use as sacrifice to the gods.

INDEX